First World War
and Army of Occupation
War Diary
France, Belgium and Germany

59 DIVISION
178 Infantry Brigade
Duke of Wellington's (West Riding Regiment)
13th Battalion
27 May 1918 - 13 September 1919

WO95/3025/10

The Naval & Military Press Ltd
www.nmarchive.com
Published in association with The National Archives

Published by

The Naval & Military Press Ltd

Unit 10 Ridgewood Industrial Park,

Uckfield, East Sussex,

TN22 5QE England

Tel: +44 (0) 1825 749494

www.naval-military-press.com

www.nmarchive.com

This diary has been reprinted in facsimile from the original. Any imperfections are inevitably reproduced and the quality may fall short of modern type and cartographic standards.

© **Crown Copyright**
Images reproduced by permission of The National Archives, London, England, 2015.

Contents

Document type	Place/Title	Date From	Date To
Heading	WO 3025 59th 178th I.B. Duke Of Wellington's 13th Bn (West Riding Rgt) 1918 May-1919 Sep		
Heading	59th Division 178th Infy Bde Duke Of Wellington's 13th Bn (West Riding Regt) May 1918-Sep 1919		
War Diary	Vielfort	27/05/1918	31/05/1918
Heading	War Diary Of 13th G. Bn. West Riding Regt. For June 1918.		
War Diary	Bois Vielfort	01/06/1918	07/06/1918
War Diary	Bois Du Hazois	08/06/1918	15/06/1918
War Diary	Bours	16/06/1918	16/06/1918
War Diary	Fontaine-Les-Boulane	17/06/1918	29/06/1918
Heading	War Diary Of 13th West Riding Rgt. July 1918		
Miscellaneous	178th Infantry Brigade	31/07/1918	31/07/1918
War Diary	Fontaine-Les-Boulane	01/07/1918	31/07/1918
Heading	War Diary Of 13th West Riding Regiment August 1918		
War Diary	Barly	01/08/1918	01/08/1918
War Diary	Bellacourt	02/08/1918	16/08/1918
War Diary	Gouy-En-Artois	17/08/1918	21/08/1918
War Diary	Battn. H.Q. S9.d.7.2. Sheet 51B.SW	21/08/1918	21/08/1918
War Diary	Saulty	22/08/1918	23/08/1918
War Diary	Molinghem	24/08/1918	26/08/1918
War Diary	St Floris	27/08/1918	30/08/1918
War Diary	L'epinette	31/08/1918	01/09/1918
War Diary	Lestrem	02/09/1918	02/09/1918
War Diary	Pont Rochon	03/09/1918	03/09/1918
War Diary	Mioc 5.7	04/09/1918	07/09/1918
War Diary	M9d.5.3	08/09/1918	13/09/1918
War Diary	Bout Deville	14/09/1918	21/09/1918
War Diary	M14d 95 90 Map Sheet Aubers	22/09/1918	25/09/1918
War Diary	M17C 5.5	26/09/1918	29/09/1918
War Diary	Bout Deville R18C 2.8	30/09/1918	30/09/1918
Heading	War Diary Of 13th Bn. Duke Of Wellingtons West Riding Regiment For October 1918		
War Diary	R 18C 2.8 Bout Deville	01/10/1918	02/10/1918
War Diary	H 16C. 20.60	03/10/1918	03/10/1918
War Diary	H21 B 3.8	04/10/1918	08/10/1918
War Diary	I19C 85-20 Sheet 36 N.W. Bois Grenier	10/10/1918	10/10/1918
War Diary	I 20d 5.3	11/10/1918	14/10/1918
War Diary	I 27 Central	15/10/1918	15/10/1918
War Diary	Ref Sheet 36. I 23 A.6.2	16/10/1918	17/10/1918
War Diary	K 19 D 3.9	18/10/1918	18/10/1918
War Diary	R.3.b.3.7.	19/10/1918	19/10/1918
War Diary	Ref Sheet 37 1/40000 M.5 D 4.5.	20/10/1918	20/10/1918
War Diary	H.32.b.02	21/10/1918	21/10/1918
War Diary	G 24 D 4.4	22/10/1918	31/10/1918
Heading	War Diary Of 13th Duke Of Wellingtons West Riding Regt. November 1918		
War Diary	Ref Sheet 37 1/40000 G 24 D 4.4	01/11/1918	08/11/1918
War Diary	Chateau I.19.b	09/11/1918	09/11/1918
War Diary	J 12 D 0.9.	10/11/1918	10/11/1918

War Diary	L 4a 9.8	11/11/1918	12/11/1918
War Diary	J 18 D.8.6	13/11/1918	15/11/1918
War Diary	H 26 B 6.6	16/11/1918	16/11/1918
War Diary	M.5 D 4.1	17/11/1918	17/11/1918
War Diary	Ref Sheet 36 1/40000 Q 22c 5.7	18/11/1918	03/12/1918
War Diary	Ref Sheet 44 K.20.a.0.2	04/12/1918	08/12/1918
War Diary	Sheet 19 N.W. H.I.C.4.4	09/12/1918	31/01/1919
War Diary	Sheet 19 N.W.	01/02/1919	28/02/1919
Heading	59 Division 178 Infy Bde Duke Of Wellington's 13th Bn (West Riding Regt) March April 1919 Missing		
War Diary	Sheet 19 N.W.	01/05/1919	31/05/1919
Heading	59 Division 178 Infy Bde Duke Of Wellington's 13th Bn (West Riding Regt) June 1919 Missing		
Heading	WO95/2488 3N 1490		
Miscellaneous	Herewith Find War Diaries For Month Of July 1919.	14/08/1919	14/08/1919
War Diary	Sheet 19 N.W.	01/07/1919	31/07/1919
Miscellaneous	The Secretary War Office (S.D.2)	01/09/1919	01/09/1919
War Diary	Sheet 19 N.W.	01/08/1919	31/08/1919
War Diary	Dunkirk Sheet 19 N.W.	01/09/1919	13/09/1919

WO 3025

59th 178th I.B.

Duke of Wellington's
13th Bn (West Riding Rgt)

1918 May – 1919 Sep

59TH DIVISION
178TH INFY BDE

DUKE OF WELLINGTON'S
13TH BN (WEST RIDING REGT)

MAY 1918 – SEP 1919

FORMED IN FRANCE

Army Form C. 2118.

WAR DIARY
or
INTELLIGENCE SUMMARY.

(Erase heading not required.)

Place	Date	Hour	Summary of Events and Information	Remarks and references to Appendices
VIELFORT	May 19th 27th		**13th Garrison Guard Battalion West Riding Regiment** Commanded by Lieut Col J.C. TABOR. The Battalion has redesignated and formed from the late 3rd Provisional Garrison Guard Battalion and forms part of the 176th Infantry Brigade - 59th Division (temporarily attached to the 177th Inf. Brigade) and is composed of the following units 243 Area Employment (Garrison Guard) Company (now A Coy) under the command of Capt W.J MELVIN - 4th ROYAL SCOTS, with the following officers Lieut J W LEES — 1st KOSB " J P BICKNELL — 2/5th BEDFORDSHIRE REGT 2nd Lieut W P DOYLE — A & S.H. " P de V ANNESLEY — LABOUR CORPS " — do Strength 222 O/Rs. 866 A.E. (G.G.) Coy under the command of Lieut HAS WALTER - R.N.V.R. with the following officers. Lieut W.GROVE PRICE — MUNSTER FUSILIERS " W MILL — 7th CAMERON HIGHLANDERS 2nd Lieut J.M RALPH — LABOUR CORPS " T OLIVER — do Strength 225 O/Rs 894 A.E. (GG) Coy under the command of Major J. CHADWICK - BUCKS BATTN with the following officers Capt R.D.E. ROBERTS — R.F.A Lieut R.A. CONNOR — " " H.S. GILBERY — " 2nd Lieut J.H DAWSON — LABOUR CORPS " J.M CANT — " " H. PYBURN — "	Sheet 44 B

WAR DIARY
or
INTELLIGENCE SUMMARY.

Army Form C. 2118.

Place	Date	Hour	Summary of Events and Information	Remarks and references to Appendices
VIEL FORT	May 1918 27th		Strength 221 O/Rs 2nd Lieut S.R. ALLSOPP LABOUR CORPS " W.J. LANGMAID " 935 A.E. (98) Coy. under the command of Major G.F.L. CLAYTON EAST - R.F.A with the following officers Lieut A.W. INGHAM KRRC 2nd Lieut H.N. FREEMAN LABOUR CORPS " J.P.R. GOLIGHTLY " " H.E. HYDE " " J.J. MCINTYRE " Strength 216 O/Rs Headquarters Lieut Colonel J.C. TABOR 8th ESSEX REGT. Capt. & Adjutant C.R. WELLS 14th DLI M.O. Capt J. FORSYTH C.A.M.C. Lieut & QM M.C. KERR 9th CAMERON HIGHLANDERS Strength 25 O/Rs	Sheet 44B
"	28/31st		The Battalion was occupied in digging the trenches at the B.B defence line in the vicinity of Short no 36 B-J13 to J20. In the event of the B.B line being recaptured the Battalion will move to a position of readiness East of the Scherpenberg and under the Rise no J32 to ready to move on orders from the 177th Bde. Digging from 6:30 A.M until tasks allotted by R.E's complete. One hour's - from 5:30 to 6:30 pm - training carried out daily.	R.W R.W J.C. Tabor /M Colonel 18" Rg a 3rd Garrison Regiment

CONFIDENTIAL

WAR DIARY

OF

13th G. Bn West Riding Regt.

FOR

JUNE 1918.

13th Bn
West Riding Regt

WAR DIARY
or
INTELLIGENCE SUMMARY.
(Erase heading not required.)

Army Form C. 2118.

June 1918

Place	Date	Hour	Summary of Events and Information	Remarks and references to Appendices
BOIS DU VIELFORT	June 1918 1st		Captain H.C. FEIN- 5th K.R.R.C. reported for duty and is taken on the strength of the Battalion. This officer is suffering from severe shell shock and is being left under observation by the M.O. for a two days. In consequence of the redesignation of the Battalion, Companies have been redesignated as follows:- 898 Area Garr. Employment Coy. 'A' Coy Platoons 1-4 866 . . . . . B . . 5-8 894 . . . . . C . . 9-12 935 . . . . . D . . 13-16	Sheet 44.B. J26.C.07
	2/3rd		Trench digging and one Rounds training carried out.	R.W. Rw.
do	4th		Trench digging and training	
			At 12.15 A.M. Hostile enemy aircraft dropped 5 bombs (at dusk) in the immediate vicinity of the camp, killing 3 men and wounding 2 men. Burial took place at BRUAY CEMETERY at 3 p.m. Capt. H.C. FEIN evacuated to C.C.S.	Shell hole nr 44.B. J.8.a. Rw
do	5th		Trench digging training carried out.	
			Trench digging carried out in the morning. In the afternoon the Battn. moved to a new location at I.35 + 4.B. (BOIS DU HAZOIS) The question of obtaining water is a serious one.	Sheet 44.B. Rw "Bw
BOIS DU VIELFORT	6/7th		Trench digging on a new scheme line at I.30-36 - J31	
	8th		Lieut. W. MILL appointed Battalion Evacuation Officer	
BOIS DU HAZOIS	9th		The Brigade manned the B.B line and the 13th(S) Batt. West Riding Regt. acting as skeleton. The Battalion was examined by Lieut Col. PRESCOTT - Inspector of Drafts. (A draft of 47 O.R.s arrived	Rw
do	10th		2nd Lieut. J.J. McINTYRE evacuated to hospital. Lieut. R.A. CONNOR appointed Battalion Intelligence Officer. Whilst near the marsh towards 8 miles in handle area. Examined by Lieut. Col. PRESCOTT.	Rw

B.E.Br.
for't Rudniskeff

WAR DIARY
or
INTELLIGENCE SUMMARY.

(Erase heading not required.)

Army Form C. 2118.

-2-

June 1918

Instructions regarding War Diaries and Intelligence
Summaries are contained in F. S. Regs., Part II.
and the Staff Manual respectively. Title pages
will be prepared in manuscript.

Place	Date 1918	Hour	Summary of Events and Information	Remarks and references to Appendices
BOIS DU HAZOIS	June 11th		Summary of the last Part the Battalion was broken up to the War Establishment of a Service Battalion. 2nd Lieut. J.P.R GOUGHTY attached Transfer to the Battalion	RW
"	12th		Capt. J FORSYTH CAMC evacuated to hospital	RW
"	13th		Trench digging and training	RW
"	14th		A.F.G.C.M held in Camp on No 471220 Pte J. DUNN on a charge of absence without leave	RW
"	15th		Trench digging and training	RW
BOURS	16th		The Battalion moved off at 7.45 AM via BURTON - DIEVAL to BOURS where it billeted for the night in which from this date the Battalion rehearsed from the 177th & 178th Infantry Bde (Commanded by Genl Col G.A. DUNCAN. M.C)	RW Sheet map nº 44 B
FONTAIN-LES-BOULANE	17th		March continued and the Batn moved off at 6.30 AM to FONTAINE-LES BOULANE via TANGRY FIEFS. Three epidemic measles and mumps Evils. The HQ of the 178th Inf Bde are in FONTAINE-LES-BOULANE. The Battalion marched in at 4 AM and the day rested. Capt. A.W. WEBB C.F. joined the unit. no strength.	do LENS 11 RW
do	18th		The Battalion is to be reorganized unopposed with G.H.Q letter AG/4176(0) d/ 8.4.18 establishment.	RW
do	19th		Inclement weather prevented training being carried out Capt S.H. KINGSTON R.A.M.C. in temporary stood for duty	RW
do	20th		The Battn is suffering from a malignant fever which appears to be epidemic and 21 ORs have been sent to hospital. Lieut. H.A.S. WALTER R.W.R evacuated to hospital	RW
do	21st		The Battalion was inspected at work by the Sgth Divisional Commander, Major General Sir R.D. WHIGHAM KCB, DSO. 2/Lieut J W RALPH evacuated to hospital with 1 o/R with Spanish fever. CAPT S.H. KINGSTON R.A.M.C evacuated to hospital and on relieved by CAPT F.J. WHITELAW, R.A.M.C	RW
do	22nd		13 O/Rs evacuated to hospital with this 3 day - fever.	RW
do	23rd		Three cases of measles have broken out amongst the children of the village 13 o/Rs evacuated today to hospital	RW

13 G.B. West Riding Regt WAR DIARY or INTELLIGENCE SUMMARY.

Army Form C. 2118.

June 1918

—3—

Place	Date	Hour	Summary of Events and Information	Remarks and references to Appendices
FONTAINE – LES – BOULANS	June 1918 24th		Lieut MILL W. and 15. O/Rs evacuated to hospital.	Sheet LENS 11 R.W.
	25th		The x Corps Commander, Lieut Gen Sir W.E. PEYTON, KCB, KCVO, DSO inspected the Battalion. 49 O/Rs (B III and B II) returned to Base.	Ross. R.W.
	26th		58 O/Rs (B I) arrived Base.	
	29th		Inspection of the Battalion by Lieut Col. H.A FULTON. D.S.O (Acting Brigadier General). The b/m officers reported for duty, and one below on the strength.	
			Capt H.K.C. HARE — 7th Yorks Regt	
			Lieut E.D. CLARK — "	
			2nd " A. FAIRBAIRNS — 10th "	
			" P. HARGREAVES — 3rd "	
			" W.S. MARRABLE — N.F.	
			" J.W. BELL — 4th Yorks Regt	
			" H.P. STYRING — "	
			" H.F. DENTON — "	
			" F. POOLE — "	
			All these officers are marked "A"	R.W.

T.C. Tabor M.C.
Cmdg 13th Garrison Bn West
Riding Regt.

CONFIDENTIAL

WAR DIARY

OF

13" West Riding Rgt.

July 1918.

A 1/20

H.Q.
178th Infantry Brigade
_____

Herewith Army Form C 2118
for the month of July 18

P.S. Clarkson Lieut Col.
13th Bn West Riding Regt

31.7.18

Army Form C. 2118.

WAR DIARY
or
INTELLIGENCE SUMMARY.
(Erase heading not required.)

JULY 1918

Instructions regarding War Diaries and Intelligence Summaries are contained in F. S. Regs., Part II. and the Staff Manual respectively. Title pages will be prepared in manuscript.

Place	Date 1918	Hour	Summary of Events and Information	Remarks and references to Appendices
FONTAINELES. BOULOGNE	July 1st		Strength of the Battalion 39 Officers, 877 O.Rs. The following vehicles and animals arrived today and are taken on the strength:- (4 in lieu of field kitchens) 10 G.S. limbered wagons, 2 H.D Horses, 12 L.D Mules	LENS. 11 Rw
"	2nd		Nowhere: 1 HD horse handed over to the 2/6 D.L.I (176th Infantry Brigade)	Rw
"	3rd		Short route march (about 6 miles) carried out. 4 HD Horses arrived from BOULOGNE.	Rw
"	4th		The Revd Capt W.E.B.B returned from leave. Training carried out.	Rw
"	5th		Lieut N. GROVE PRICE proceeded to ENGLAND on 14 days leave. Notification received that CAPT I.T.C FEIN KRRC had been invalided to ENGLAND and is accordingly struck off the Strength of the Battalion.	Rw
"	6th		Training carried out. 2/Lts L.J. McIntyre + J.W. Ralph reported from hospital.	H.P.
"	7th		Draft of 50 O.Rs arrived (Signallers + Bn P.T Instructor.)	H.P.
"	8th		F.S.C.M. held at Lines on 411260 Pte McGee G. and 42650 Pte Abrahams H. Capt F.K. Marriott R.A.M.C. reported for duty. Lt Whitelaw returned to 2/377 N.M.F.A.	H.P.
"	9th		Bn. inspection on parade ground by Divl Commander + A.D.M.S. Captain men recommended for further inspection. Lt Mill returned from hospital. Adjt left on 14 days leave to U.K. H.P. 2nd Lt L.J. McIntyre evacuated to hospital.	
"	10th		Training. Lt Kees rejoining from Mitrailleuse School - J.D. Bryden Yorks Rgt" reported for duty.	H.P.

Army Form C. 2118.

WAR DIARY
or
INTELLIGENCE SUMMARY.
(Erase heading not required.)

Instructions regarding War Diaries and Intelligence Summaries are contained in F. S. Regs., Part II. and the Staff Manual respectively. Title pages will be prepared in manuscript.

Place	Date 1918	Hour	Summary of Events and Information	Remarks and references to Appendices Lens II
Fontinettes - Les - Boulogne	July 11th		Major J. Chadwick went on leave. Div' Commander A.D.M.S. visited B'n. Inspector of drafts examined men unfit to go into trenches in great part of line & many of all B.11 men the P. Hospital evacuated to Hospital	H.P.
"	12th		Inspector of drafts completed examination of B'n. 234 men marked B.11 and 40 men marked B.111 Lt. W. Ingham granted leave to U.K. Lot Debot appointed at Bde Commander. Capt. H.K.C. Hone of C.O.	H.P.
"	13th		Training. Battalion inspected at Pucdasfin by Gen. Sir H.S. Horne K.C.B. 1st Army Commander. demonstration to Offs. & N.C.O.s at Pucdasfin by platoon J.H.A.C. Capt. Melvin, 2/Lt's Elvin and Annesley went to Base for M.B. L's Harnett reported for duty.	H.P.
"	14th		New Reg't Nos. Offices and O.R.s classified B.II + B.III by I.D. warned to "Stand to"	H.P.
"	15th		Training	H.P.
"	16th		Training	H.P.
"	17th		5 Offices + 271 O.R.s proceeded to Base. Lt J.W. Aus. Lt. to Mill. Lt. W.P. Doyle 2/Lt H.E. Hyde and 2/Lt. W.S.J. Langmaid.	H.P.
"	18th/20		Training and reorganisation	Rls.

WAR DIARY
or
INTELLIGENCE SUMMARY.
(Erase heading not required.)

Army Form C. 2118.

Place	Date	Hour	Summary of Events and Information	Remarks and references to Appendices
FONTAINE-LES-BOULANE.	1918 July 21st		Major J.A. RODDICK, 1/10th Bn. Scottish K.L.R. reported for duty and assumed command of the Battalion vice Lieut Col. J.C. TABOR.	R.W.
"	22nd		Lieut B.H. BREWILL 2/6 Sherwood Foresters attached for duty as Sanitation Officer. Orders received that the Battalion was under Commenc to the BARLY Army Area.	R.W.
"	23rd		The Battalion entrained as part of 178th Bn Bde at ₤ L II d.4.3. (FONTAINE-LES-BOULANE-HEUCHIN Road) and moved to BARLY via ANVIN-ST. POL-ROULLECOURT-TERNAS-AVESNES-le-COMTE. The Battn detrained at 1. PM at ₤ L II d.4.3 (FONTAINE-LES-BOULANE) P.10.c.g.I. (BARLY-FOSSEUX Rd) at 6 PM. The Battn occupied Billets in BARLY. Lt-Col J.C. TABOR detached for temporary instruction to the 20th Division. Lieut Col P.M. STEVENSON D.S.O. 2nd K.O.S.B. assumed command of the Battalion. 25 O/Rs (BII) proceeded to Base.	Sheet 44C Sheet 51C R.W.
	24th		The Commanding officer, Adjutant and all officers visited the PURPLE system of trenches in the BLAIREVILLE area. The HQ of the 178th Inf Bde is situated in BARLY. The Battalion now is in the XVII Corps of the III Army	R.W.
	25th		The Commanding officer held a conference to discuss the question of reorganisation. The GO instructs the Battalion.	R.W.
	26th		Adjutant (Capt. C.R. WELLS) returned from leave. 2nd Lieut H.P. HARGREAVES returned from hospital.	R.W.
	27th		Training Carried out.	R.W.
	28th		A draft of 280 O/Rs arrived from the Divisional Reception Camp. Intimation received that Lieut W.C.RAVE-PRICE returning from leave and proceeded to Base from the Reception Camp.	R.W.
	29th		Draft inducted by 9OC 178 Inf Bn Bde and allotted to Companies. Major J CHADWICK returned from leave.	R.W.
	30th		The Battalion inspected by the Divisional Commander and A.D.M.S. examined new draft and BII Category men; also 6 officers. Were taken on the strength of the Battalion. The following officers reported and were taken on the strength of the Battalion. 2/Lt TURNBULL R.J. DLI " TURNER H.T. " " PURCIFER T.R. " " HUNTLEY A " " BRISTOW H "	R.W.
	31st		2/Lt A.W. INGHAM returned from leave.	R.W.

P. Stg??
Cmd'g 1/5th W.Yorks R.

Confidential

War Diary

of

13th West Riding Regiment

August 1918.

Confidential

WAR DIARY

August 1918 13 York Riding Regt. Army Form C. 2118.

INTELLIGENCE SUMMARY.

(Erase heading not required.)

Place	Date 1918	Hour	Summary of Events and Information	Remarks and references to Appendices
BARLY	Aug 1st		Strength of the Battn 32 Officers, 902 O/Rs. Battalion inspected by the XI Corps Commander Lieut Gen Sir Ingham Haldane K.C.B, D.S.O. Personnel received by the Commander at the range. Through a defective cartridge the bolt head of the rifle belonging to No 43376 Pte DALE.E. striking him in the temple. Major J. CHADWICK detached for the Sqt. Divisional Reception Camp.	Sheet Ref 51 C RW

BELLACOURT	"2nd"		The following Officers and other ranks appointed for the Base on the authority of the ADMS
			2/Lt BICKNELL J.P.C.
			  " CANT S.M.
			  " ALLSOPP S.R.
			  " PYBURN H
			  " GOLIGHTLY J.P.R
			  " HARGREAVES P
			and 44 O/Rs
			The Battalion moved to BELLACOURT by route march and took over the billets of the 11th Bn Somerset Light Infantry. The 178th Inf. Bde have taken over the right section of the Divisional front (Sheet 51 B.S.W. 1/20000. Right S.12.d.1.9. Left Boundary M.36.c.0.0.) and the Battn is in Brigade Reserve
				Sheet Ref 51 C
				RW
				RW

	3/5th		Training carried out extending the relief of Reserves	

	6th		The Divisional Commander inspected the Battalion at training
			The following Officers are posted and taken on the strength of the Battn.
			  Capt BARBER A. M.C. 2/6 Sherwood Foresters (attached 178th Inf. Bde Staff)
			  " WHEATLAND A.S.
			  " DOND R.H.
			  2nd Lieut STRONG C.F.
			  Lieut BRENELL B.H. 1/8th Bn. Essex Regt.; Capt WHEATLAND A.S. 55th Div School	

	7/9th		The following Officers rejoined to duty and are taken on the strength of the Battn.
			  2nd Lieut JOHNS T.F. } Yorkshire Regt
			  " GODFREY P.J. } Reported on the 8th
			  " HANSON J.S.
			Training carried out.
				RW

WAR DIARY or INTELLIGENCE SUMMARY.

Army Form C. 2118.

B. Yorkshire Reg.t

August 1918

Place	Date	Hour	Summary of Events and Information	Remarks and references to Appendices

BELLACOURT	August 9th		Continued. 2nd Lieut. LAMB J.A. 4th W.YORKS) Reported on the 8th
			      " MARSHALL H.C.) 3rd W.R.R.
			      " HODGSON S.L.) " " " - 9th
			      " MOORE J.L.)
			      " OLDROYD F.)
			Lieut. Col. P.H.STEVENSON D.S.O. proceeded to the U.K. on Special Leave for 14 days. Major J.A. RODDICK M.C. assumed command.
				R.W.

"	10		A.D.M.S. classified 5/6 O/Rs N.B.I.	R.W.
"	11		Lieut A.W.INGHAM proceeded to the Base on the authority of the A.D.M.S. for the purposes of Metrification.	R.W. R.W.
"	12		5/6 O/Rs B II. transferred to the Base.	R.W.
"	13/14		The Patrol returned to the 36th N.F. in the BRICKFIELDS System at enemy front line. The Batt. commenced moving from BELLACOURT at 8 p.m. and the relief was completed by 12.35 a.m. This is the first time the Batt. had been in the trenches since its demob. Night very quiet. The 1st Guards Brigade raided the enemy front at S.24.a.5.4. Zero hour being 2.30 a.m. Aug 14th. Artillery fire commenced at zero and ceased at zero plus 20 mins. Quiet night on. Wind S.W. 10 m.p.h.	Sheet 57.6.S.W. S.2.b.5.1. R.W.
"	15		Slight shelling during morning at night. No casualties.	R.W.
"	16		Quiet day and night. Calm intelligence indicates favourable withdrawal or unusual Property	R.W.
"	17/18		Quiet day and night. Relieved on the night of 17/18 by the 1st Batt. ESSEX REGt. 17th Infantry Brigade. Relief completed in two hours. The Battalion moved to GOUY-EN-ARTOIS where it occupied billets	R.W.
GOUY-EN-ARTOIS	19		Inspection and organizing Companies was carried on	R.W.
"	20		Capt. H.C.HARE detailed off to Hospital. Lt. J.F.JOHN's assumed command of B Coy.	R.W.
"	21		Lt. R.A.CONNOR. Granted leave to UK. for 14 days. The Batt. debussed at 6 p.m. and Orders received in the afternoon to embus for BLAIREVILLE. The Batt. debussed at 6 p.m. and at 8.45 p.m. moved forward to the front line and relieved the 1st Batt. GRENADIER GUARDS - 3rd	R.W.

August 1918 1/5th West Riding Regt

WAR DIARY
or
INTELLIGENCE SUMMARY.
(Erase heading not required.)

Instructions regarding War Diaries and Intelligence Summaries are contained in F.S. Regs., Part II. and the Staff Manual respectively. Title pages will be prepared in manuscript.

Army Form C. 2118.

Place	Date 1918	Hour	Summary of Events and Information	Remarks and references to Appendices
Batt. HQ Sq. 7.2 Sheet 51 B.S.W.	Aug 21st		2nd GUARDS BRIGADE, on the right flank of the 59th Divisional Front; the 1st IRISH GUARDS being on the right of the Battn. The relief was conducted by 12.45 am. No casualties. Night quiet with very bright moonlight. 2/Lt H.P. DENTON was left out of the trenches as 1st Details.	Rw
SAULTY	22/8		2/Lt J.S. HANSON proceeded on leave to U.K. Enemy attacked on our right flank at 5 am. but was repulsed. Shrapnel fire with S.O.S. gun shells (Blue Cross) and T.M. carried out harassing fire during the day. Warning Order re Conference at 4.10 pm of the relief by the 4th Battn LONDON REGT - 56th Division. The HQ 168 Infy Brigade occupied Battn HQ at 10.30 p.m. The relief by the 4th LONDON REGT commenced at 11.30 pm. Enemy was confirmed completed until 3.45 a.m. Harassing fire was carried on continuously during the relief. The Battalion concentrated and bivouacked in the BLAMONT MILL area. At 4.45 a.m. the 168th Infy Bde advanced to attack: BOYELLES being the line of a limited objective. This was gained. At 5.15 p.m. the Battalion moved to SAULTY area and bivouaces for the night.	Rw
MOLINGHEM	24th		The Battn entrained at LARBRET Sidings at 11.42 A.M. destination unknown. Attached the Transport who marched by road to WAIL. Detrained at BERGUETTE at 5 p.m. and marched to MOLINGHEM where the Battn remained billeted.	Sheet 36A Rw
	25/8		Inspection and organising carried on. The O.C. on having inspection of the Battn taken by the Battn for the relief by the 4th Battn LONDON REGT, and the manner in which they were quartered out. An Advance Party of C.O. Intelligence, OC Coy went forward to reconnoitre the line. The Battn will probably move forward tomorrow. Transport arrived in the night of the 25/26 2/Lt Col P.H STEVENSON returned from leave.	Rw
ST FLORIS	27		Operation Orders issued yesterday. The Battn paraded at MOLINGHEM at 2.00 and 4.30 am and detrained at ST VENANT and relieved the 15th ESSEX REGT - 177 Infantry Bde in Reserve line - Battn H.Q. Location (S36a) P5d 1.6 Relief completed by 7.26 p.m. 2/Lt J.W. BELL evacuated to hospital. Night quiet	Rw Ref Sheet 36A 1/40.000 Rw

August 1/1918   13th West Riding Regt

WAR DIARY
INTELLIGENCE SUMMARY

Army Form C. 2118.

Place	Date 1918	Hour	Summary of Events and Information	Remarks and references to Appendices
ST FLORIS	Aug 28		2/Lt T A LAMB granted leave to U.K. from 29-8-18 to 12-9-18. Quiet day and night.	RW
	29		A fatigue party of 50 prisoners from Pards totalling 60 employed under Divisional Agricultural Officer in harvesting & threshing fonageration. The G.O.C. 178th Infty Bde held a Conference at 11 A.M. with C.O. Scouts in Command, Adjutant and O.C. Coys on the subject of an advance with the enemy withdrawing on the Brigade front. Court of Enquiry held on the absence of No. 49500 Pte TRIGG. G. who was found when apprehended. President Capt FATHERSON - Members 2/Lt J HODGSON and 2/Lt P J GODFREY	RW
	30		2/Lt A FAIRBAIRN assumes command of D Coy. vice Lt J.D. BRYDEN proceeded to HYTHE for Musketry Course. 2/Lt H.P. STYRING proceeds to S.E. Army Signion Course. - " - 2/Lt P J GODFREY - " - Musketry	RW
L'EPINETTE	31		2/Lt H F DENTON attended F.G.C.M at interning ASYLUM, ST. VENANT as witness. The Battalion moved to L'EPINETTE area and took over a line from MELVILLE to L'EPINETTE and day billeted as in. 16 Battln of Battn H.Q. A, B & C & T.R. The 177th Bn. Bde are at present in the front line in position of Reserve.	Sketch 36.A.S.E. Appendix R W

(J Shutner) RSM
C Sgt 13 Wd Riding

13th West Riding Regt

WAR DIARY
INTELLIGENCE SUMMARY.

Army Form C. 2118.

Sept 1918

Place	Date 1918	Hour	Summary of Events and Information	Remarks and references to Appendices
L'EPINETTE	Sept 1st		The Batt. moved on to the vicinity of L'EPINETTE and occupied a line of shell holes from L'EPINETTE inclusive to the CANAL (exclusive) (MEDRILLON) in support to the 177th Infy Bde. Batt H.Q. location Q 5 d 7 8. 2/Lt. H. DENTON attached additional on a Cadre hosted at the G.H.Q. course of B.F.& P.T. 2/Lt A. HUNTLY proceeded to the G.H.Q. course of B.F.& P.T. The night was quiet but rain fell heavily.	reports Shell 36 A 5 E
				RW
LESTREM	2nd		The 13th WRR relieved the 11th SOMERSET LIGHT INFANTRY in the front line LESTREM area. Relief completed at 10 p.m. Batt H.Q. located at R 10 a 5.8. Lt BRENNAN, 2/Lt HARRISON, 2/Lt. WEST RIDING REGT joined the Batt. Slight shelling took place during the night - no casualties. 2/Lt H.Q. 27236 Pte DURKIN - M enlisted in a German steel boots Batt. left whilst wiring off from L'EPINETTE H.Q. 27236 Pte DURKIN - M killed in a German steel boots which exploded and injured him in the thigh.	(Pay)
PONT ROCHON	3rd	1 AM	Orders received that the 1/9 Durham on our right and 6th RICHEBOURG ST VAST and CROIX BARBER on our left and 36 NF to cooperate in capturing ETON HARROW and CHARTERHOUSE Posts at the same time. First objective of the latter ETON POST included; second objective HARROW and CHARTERHOUSE. Zero Hour 5.30 AM. After the capture of these Posts the 13th WR & the more forward located to the objective ESTAIRES - LA BASSEE ROAD. In conjunction with the 6 Inst Division on on the left, the Batt. pushed forward making further objectives about 12 p.m. Orders were then received to push on to the second objective LA FLINGUE 12 p.m. Orders were then received to push on to the second objective LA FLINGUE POST G C 35 C 4.1. Owing to the exhausted condition of the men and machine gun opposition it was found inadvisable to gain this end. The line rested from M19 d 9 9 to LE DRUMEZ. Casualties 30 o/r. wounded by M.G. fire. At 6.30 p.m. Batt H.Q. was moved forward to PONT ROCHON - R 5 d 2 3.	36 A 5 E and 36 N W
				Rev
M10 C 5.7	4th		The Batt. during the morning gained a line East of LAVENTIE from M 5 b 5.7 & M16 b 77 and during the evening further forward to a line running from M11 c 0.0 to M 6 d 8 k. Batt. H.Q. moved forward to M10 C 5.7. The 25 Batt. KING'S LIVERPOOLS relieved the Batt. by taking up a line in front even the Batt. remained about half an hour armed in support. Casualties 1 killed 3 wounded o/r. Pneumonia. Slight shelling during the night.	RW

13 West Riding Regt

Army Form C. 2118.

WAR DIARY
or
INTELLIGENCE SUMMARY.
(Erase heading not required.)

Title pages September 1918

Place	Date	Hour	Summary of Events and Information	Remarks and references to Appendices
LAVENTIE M10c.5.7	1918 Sept 5th		There was considerable enemy activity by the enemy during the day. Slight shelling took place. Casualties 1 O/R lightly wounded. Quiet night. The weather continues to be fine.	Rw
"	6		Capt R.A. UPTON proceeded to 5th Army School for Company Commanders Course. 2/Lt W.Coy. and 2/Lt W. FIELDEN W.R.R. joined the Bn. Gas shells fell in front of our position about 10:30 pm the alarm was given and Box Respirators worn.	Rw
"	7		Bright quiet. Casualties nil. Battn HQ heavily shelled with HE. Casualties 2 O/R killed and 2 O/Rs wounded (one at duty) Night quiet.	Rw
Mqd.5.3	8		Battn HQ moved to LA FLINGUE Cross Roads - Mqd 6.3. Intermittent hostile shelling during the night. Casualties nil.	Rw
"	9		At 6pm a heavy hostile barrage was opened on our right flank previous to a local attack by the 1/R Durham. Casualties nil. Quiet night.	Rw
"	10		2/Lieut J.W. MARRABLE evacuated to Ambulance sick. Major J.A. RODDICK proceeds to the #1 Corps Gas Course. Slight shelling during afternoon. Casual Coy 10/R killed 2 o/as wounded Lieut R.A.CONNOR rejoined from leave. Intermittent shelling during the night. The effects of being so long in still water and inclement weather is causing a great deal of sickness.	Rw
"	11		A draft of 22 O/Rs joins the Bn. 2nd Lt J.S. HANSON rejoined from leave. Casualties 2 O/Rs killed and 6 O/Rs wounded. Reconnaissance patrols operating during the night.	Rw
"	12		The 61st Division on the left flank carried out a local attack this morning. The 13th Royal Welsh Fusiliers cooperated. Casualties nil.	Rw

13 West Riding Regt
Sept 1918

Army Form C. 2118.

WAR DIARY
or
INTELLIGENCE SUMMARY.

(Erase heading not required.)

Place	Date 1918 Sept.	Hour	Summary of Events and Information	Remarks and references to Appendices
AVENTIE M9 d 5.3	13		Enemy shelled roads at intervals during the day. 2/Lt H N FREEMAN evacuated [illeg] with Chronic ill [illeg] hill. The Batt. was relieved by the 15th ESSEX REGT (2 Coys only) and relief of Coys completed at 10.30 p.m. The Batt. Concentrates at BOUT DEVILLE - Batt HQ R 18 c 2.8.	RW
BOUT DEVILLE	14		Major J A RODDICK M.C. rejoined from Course. Reinforcements to hospital from 6/13th September 94 O/Rs. Slight shelling during the evening. Casualties O/R 1 killed 1 wounded. Quiet night.	RW
	15		Enemy carried activity during the day. Hostile shelling, which included a large number of gas shells during the night.	RW
	16		Aerial activity and hostile shelling throughout the day. From 8.30 p.m. on continuously throughout the night the area was shelled with gas shells.	RW
	17		Transport moved from JESTREM to BOIST DEVILLE (Location R11 C 4.1) Hostile shelling at intervals throughout the day. 2nd Lieut HANSON T.S., 2nd Lt COY.W., Lt BRENNAN D.J. and 22 O/Rs evacuated to hospital. Arr: Capt Applies working parties for repairing roads under R.E. 2/Lt LAMB J.A. rejoined from leave. 2/Lt BELL I.W. from hospital. 2/Lt TURNBULL R.G. 2/Lt PURCIFER T.R. and 2/Lt BRISTOWE H.H. rejoined from Courses	RW
	18		Two enemy aeroplanes were reported. Lampertuire at 7.42 hours. Little hostile shelling. Gas shelling. Coy [illeg] Gas Mile.	RW
	19		Two Enemy aeroplanes on roads at morning. Casualties O/R 1 killed. Transport moved to R10 & 95.558 owing to shelling. Casualties O/R 1 wounded. 2/Lt FRICKER C.W. 3rd Batt D of W.W.R.R reported for duty night quiet.	RW

13th West Riding Regt.

Army Form C. 2118.

WAR DIARY
or
INTELLIGENCE SUMMARY.
(Erase heading not required.)

September 1918

Place	Date 1918	Hour	Summary of Events and Information	Remarks and references to Appendices
BOUT DEVILLE (HESTREM 105517)	Sept 20		Two Companies road repairing. Quiet day and night. Casualties nil. 2nd Lts GODFREY and STYRING rejoined from Course	R.W.
	21st		Two Companies road repairing. Quiet day and night. Casualties nil.	R.W.
M14 d.95.90 nr AUBERS	22nd		Heavy hostile shelling at 6 pm close to Batt HQ. The 178th Infy Bde relieves the 177th Infy Bde in the line. The 13th W.R. relieves the 2/6th Durhams Light Infantry in Brigade Reserve. Batt HQ locates M14 d 95.90. Relief completed at 10.5 pm. Hostile gas shelling of M16 & 40.10 and M16 d 30 60. Casualties nil. 2/Lt J.R RALPH proceeded to join the 198 Infan Bgd. nr attack of the Aircraft	R.W.
	23rd		Hostile shelling 5.30 am — locality shelled M 6 6 2/Lt DENTON evacuated to details 2/Lt FRICKER. Working party of 1 officer and 80 o/r under R.E. at MASSELOT POST. Enemy fairly quiet throughout the day, the hostile machine guns & snipers influence evening quiet, but hostile shelling, including gas, during the night. Casualties nil.	R.W.
	24th		F&CM on No 43299 Pte R BISSENDON took place at R.10 a 40 (H.Q.s 176 Infy Bde) and the case was adjourned. Hostile arti activity throughout the day and persistent shelling (mostly the ancient) Casualties 1 o/r wounded.	
	25th		Harassing party of 2 officers and 150 o/r under the Field Coy R.E worked late at M24 d 29 T. Heavy barrage put down by our artillery on the night of 24th/25th and lasted for about an hour, enemy rally very feeble. Gas shells on the vicinity of Batt HQ and gas & lachrymose shelling of a desultory nature in the Batt front during the day. Casualties 1 o/r killed and 1 o/r wounded	R.W.

13th West Riding Regt

WAR DIARY
or
INTELLIGENCE SUMMARY

Army Form C. 2118.

Sept 1918

Place	Date 1918	Hour	Summary of Events and Information	Remarks and references to Appendices
M.14.d.95.90 Map Sheet AUBERS	Sept 25th	11.39 p.m.	The 29th Brigade R.F.A. put down a crash on TWO TREE FARM and continued firing at a slow rate for five minutes.	
		11.40 p.m.	100 Drums C.G. were fired from projectors from M.6.d.5.4 - target area N.1.d.5.5. Enemy retaliated strongly with yellow and Blue Cross gas shells. About 100 of these fell in the vicinity of A Coy. HQ compelling them to move to M.6.a.4.3. An extensive bombardment in region of RED HOUSE M.6.d.2.0 at 12.40 A.M. accompanied by increased activity on the part of our artillery. No enemy reply. 2nd Lt FAIRBAIRNS wounded for the REST HOUSE - PARIS PLACE.	Rw
M.17.c.5.5.	26th		Day quiet. Hostile aerial activity at 5 p.m. The Batt relieved the 11th ROYAL SCOTS FUSILIERS (two one-company) in the Right Sub Sector B.C. and B Coys in the front line with A Coy in Right Support and D Coy RSF in left support. Relief completed at 2.25 A.M. 27th Sept. Hostile and gas shelling during evening and slight shelling during the night. Casualties nil. 2nd Lt T.R. PURCIFER evacuated to hospital.	Rw
	27th		Quiet day and night. Shelling with 1 O/R went out at midnight to inspect the enemy's wire; returned at 2.45 A.M. 28th Sept. Casualties nil. 2nd Lt W.S. MARRABLE evacuated to ENGLAND and no strength of the Batt.	R.W.
	28th		Slight hostile shelling during the morning on the Batt front. Casualties 2 O/R killed 4 O/R wounded. Heavy hostile shelling at 10 p.m.; a large number of shells falling in the vicinity of Batt HQ. The activity throughout the night. The Divisional Commander has heated commendation for the following Officers who have been wounded of recent dates Capt. W. FAIRCLARKE, Lt E.A.C. JOHNS and 2nd Lt A FAIRBAIRNS.	Rw

12 West Riding Regt

WAR DIARY
or
INTELLIGENCE SUMMARY

Sept 1918

Army Form C. 2118.

Place	Date 1918	Hour	Summary of Events and Information	Remarks and references to Appendices
M17 c 5.5	Sept. 29		Worked shelling during the day. Quiet night. Rain fell heavily. Casualties 1 O.R. killed, 3 O/Rs Officers and 4 o/R wounded	R.W.
BOUT DEVILLE R18 C 2.8	30th		The Batt. were by the 11th ROYAL SCOTS FUSILIERS and B C D Coys moved into Outpost line of Resrve coming under the command of the 11th R.S.F. HQ and A Coy moved to BOUT DEVILLE area. Relief completed by 3.45 AM. Casualties nil. At 7.30 this morning the 11th R.S.F. in conjunction with the 1st Division attacked and it is reported that all objectives were gained. Strength of the Batt. 36 OFFICERS and 674 O/Rs	R.W.

(J Stephenson) Lt Col.
Cmdg 13 W. Riding Regt.

Confidential.

WAR DIARY

OF

5th Bn Duke of Wellington's
West Riding Regiment.

for

October 1918

Army Form C. 2118.

WAR DIARY
or
INTELLIGENCE SUMMARY. 13 Bathn of Yorkshire

(Erase heading not required.)

Place	Date	Hour	Summary of Events and Information	Remarks and references to Appendices
R 18 C 2.8 BOUT DEVILLE	OCT 1918 1		Lt Col P.H. STEVENSON. D.S.O. relinquished command of the Battalion and proceeded to DIEPPE for the purpose of examination & medical leaving Board. Lt P.S. HALL - DSO WEST YORKS assumed command. Lt J BRENNAND and 2/Lt H. DENTON rejoined from hospital. The day has been devoted to organising and cleaning up. Strength 37 Officers 670 O/Rs	RW
"	2		The Bn intended to attack to the 173rd Infantry Brigade. That 173 Bde relieved the 182nd Sup Bde in Left Section of 61st Divisional front on night 2/3rd October. Capt F.A. UPTON rejoined from course of instruction. 2/Lt J.L. MOORE rejoined from hospital.	RW
H16.e.20.60	3		The Bn when required at 09.00 by route march to Square H31a (Sheet 36) and rested here for 1 hour. The head was continued at 04.15 to H16 e 20.60 where the Bn bivouaced in old GERMAN trenches. Transport located at H21 a 3.6. The Bn came under the orders of the 178 Infty Bde again. Arrangements made for Bombing have been located, especially in the vicinity of roads.	RW
H21 to 3.6	4		Morning devoted to clearing of trenches found open. Batt HQ moved to H21 & 3.8. 2/Lt J.H. BELL evacuated to hospital and 2/Lt G.W. FRICKER rejoined from hospital.	RW
	5		Hostile aircraft flew over the area during the afternoon and morning 2/Lt P.J. GODFREY proceeded home to UK.	RW
	6/p		Company training Carried out special attention be given to the training of Lewis Gunners	RW

Army Form C. 2118.

WAR DIARY
or
INTELLIGENCE SUMMARY.   13 Duke of Wellington's

(Erase heading not required.)

Instructions regarding War Diaries and Intelligence Summaries are contained in F. S. Regs., Part II. and the Staff Manual respectively. Title pages will be prepared in manuscript.

Place	Date	Hour	Summary of Events and Information	Remarks and references to Appendices
H21 & 6 FLEURBAIX	Oct 1918 8		The Battalion paraded this morning for the Investiture of MM to No 213416 Cpl. F HENRY and No 43178 Pte. E.J. PRICE by the Divisional Commander. The awards were gained during the advance on LAVENTIE for gallantry and devotion to duty. The following reinforcements arrived to day:- Lieut. T.Q.M. SAUNDERS F.M. Pool of Quartermasters 2nd Lieut. FAWCETT I.M. } from base W.R. Regt. do TUDD W.W. do HOBSON L. and 65 O/Rs from base	RW
I19c85-20 Sheet 36 NW BOIS GRENIER	10th		The draft was inoculated this morning by the Divisional Commander No 43278 Pte R. BISSENDEN tried by F.G.C.M. for writing letter of threatening nature. The 178th Infy Bde relieved the 177th Infy Bde in the night. Disposition of the Divisional front. Then Batt. relieved the 11th Somerset L.I. and went into support at 2am Batt. H.Q. I19 c 85.20 left Brigade Boundary grid jus Eastwards from 120 centre. Int. Batt Boundary line drawn due East through I25c0.5. Dispositions: 2 companies in front line Aystan and two in Artillery support 1 HOBSON evacuated to hospital 2nd Lieut W. ROSIE reported for duty Casualties 2 O/A wounded. Quiet Night.	RW
I20d 6.3.	11th		Batt HQ (I20d 5.3.) moved to a more sheltered location. 2 Lieut HARRISON - A Coy - East out patrol during which Lewis gun team on left Coy front. Hostile MG very active on front and left flank 2 Lieut ROSIE - C Coy - Took out a patrol but were unable to advance owing to hostile artillery fire. Casualties 5 O/Rs wounded.	RW
T20 d 5.3	12th		Heavy shelling by enemy from 0100 to day break. Patrols were sent out during the night. The day passed quietly except for slight enemy shelling in the evening increasing in activity during the night. Casualties 2 O/Rs Killed & 1 O/R wounded.	W.L.F.

Army Form C. 2118.

WAR DIARY
or
INTELLIGENCE SUMMARY.
(Erase heading not required.)

1st Duke of Wellington's

Place	Date	Hour	Summary of Events and Information	Remarks and references to Appendices
I.20.d.5.3	1918 Oct 13th		Situation quiet up to 16.15. Hostile Shelling in the evening. Strong reply from our batteries. Operation Orders No 14 Ref Sheet 36 N.W.4 and ammunition orders issued.	W.D.3
I.20.d.5.3	14th		The Battalion sent out patrols at 05.00. The RADINGHEM RIDGE South of WEZ MACQUART (Reference Sheet 36 NE) was taken and 17 prisoners and one Machine Gun Captured before noon. Also more prisoners were captured of the Kaiser Karl Regiment but we had not sufficient men to send them back. In face of strong opposition by enemy our men had to withdraw to old position of it being three times counter attacked. At 11.45 – 12.15 our artillery put up a strong barrage. One of our Airmen brought down. Casualties Killed:– Captain Fairbairn A. & 2/Lt Laund J.A. and 4 O.R's. Wounded:– 12 O.R's Missing:– Lt Priday H.E.L. and 5 O.R's missing. 2/Lt Rosie W. 2/Lt Tricker G.W. and 4 O.R's gassed. A barrage was put up at 20.00 to 20.30 for the purpose of holding enemy in the trenches. Capt A Fairbairn body found. Capt B.J. Uplin proceeded to 5th Army Musketry School. Night quiet – Enemy appears to be withdrawing. His Guns = Four fires were observed near LILLE.	W.D.3
I.27 Central	15th		B Coy relieved A Coy in front line system. Hostile Shelling during the morning and in any aircraft active. 2/Lt H.C. Marshall went out with patrol to Farm I.29.c.7.7 with orders to attack back	W.D.7

Army Form C. 2118.

WAR DIARY
or
INTELLIGENCE SUMMARY.
(Erase heading not required.)

Bn Duke of Wellington's

Instructions regarding War Diaries and Intelligence Summaries are contained in F. S. Regs., Part II. and the Staff Manual respectively. Title pages will be prepared in manuscript.

Place	Date 1918	Hour	Summary of Events and Information	Remarks and references to Appendices
R4 Sheet 36. T 23 a.6.2.	Oct. 16th		Battalion H.Q. moved forward to D'HANGARDRY CASTLE. Capt. & Adjt R. Wells wounded. Battalion Congratulated by Corps Commander for work done. 2/Lt A.E. King & 2/Lt J. Seaton with 30 other ranks reported from base. Heavy trench shelling all day. Patrols sent out and reported front clear of the enemy. Operation Orders issued.	W.L.?
T 23 a.6.2.	17th		Two male civilians passed Battalion H.Q. from LILLE and were sent under escort to Brigade H.Q. The Battalion advanced to LOMME CHATEAU then on to LASSUS CHATEAU and pushed forward to LE BEL AIR. Battalion H.Q. established at K.19.d.3.9. Several civilians met - no on arrival.	W.L.?
K 19 d.3.9	18th		The Battalion pushed forward through LA MADELINE and FLERS and Battalion H.Q. was established at R.3.c.37. Heavy shelling at ANNAPLES at 17-30. During the night the Battalion was relieved by the 36th Northumberland Fusiliers 177th Inf. Brigade.	W.L.?
R.3.c.37.	19th		The Battalion marched via LA MARAIS - FARM LANGLET to FOREST LILLE arriving there about 12.00 and Battalion H.Q. was established at M 2 c 37 (Ref Sheet 37) The Battalion moved off again at 15.15 and reached WILHEMS. Battalion established at M 5 d H.S. at 1700	W.L.?

Army Form C. 2118.

WAR DIARY
or
INTELLIGENCE SUMMARY.   B" Duke of Wellington

(Erase heading not required.)

Instructions regarding War Diaries and Intelligence Summaries are contained in F. S. Regs., Part II. and the Staff Manual respectively. Title pages will be prepared in manuscript.

Place	Date 1918	Hour	Summary of Events and Information	Remarks and references to Appendices
37 1/40.000 Ref Sheet M.5.d.4.5	Oct 20th		The Battalion received orders to march to TEMPLEUVE arriving there at 1800. Battalion Head Quarters H 32.6.0.2.	W.L.7
H 32.6.0.2	21st		Hostile shelling at intervals throughout the day. The Battalion was relieved by the 1/5th Loyal North Lancashire Regt and marched to Farm G 24.d.4.4. where Batt H.Q" were established.	W.L.7
G 24.d.4.4	22nd		Day devoted to cleaning up, interior economy, and checking of Mobilisation Stores. Hostile shelling in vicinity of H.Q.	W.L.7
G 24.d.4.4	23rd		Training under Company Commanders after Schemes had been submitted to the Commanding Officer. Advances in the open practised and attention given to sending back information and keeping Aviation Commanding Officer inspected one Company and held conference with Company Commanders at 1700. Boxing & Singing competitions held in the afternoon & evening respectively.	W.L.7
G 24.d.4.4	24th		Companies paraded for inspection at 09.00. A + B Coys carried on training – Schemes having been approved by the Commanding Officer. C + D Coys carried out repair of roads at Field d.b.i. Shell Craters in G 24.d and H.19.c. The Commanding Officer inspected the Transport Section. Capt H.K.C. Have reported	W.L.7

D. D. & L., London, E.C. (A500) Wt. W7771/M2031 750,000 5/17 Sch. 52 Forms/C2118/4

Army Form C. 2118.

WAR DIARY
or
INTELLIGENCE SUMMARY.
(Erase heading not required.)

Bn Duke of Wellington's

Instructions regarding War Diaries and Intelligence Summaries are contained in F. S. Regs., Part II. and the Staff Manual respectively. Title pages will be prepared in manuscript.

Place	Date	Hour	Summary of Events and Information	Remarks and references to Appendices
Ref Sheet 37 1/40000	1918 Oct 24		(Contd) from Hospital and took over Command of "B" Company. Operation Orders No 15 issued at 18.15". Singing Competition held in the evening.	b. b. 2
G.24 d u 4	25th		Companies paraded at 0900 for inspection. B+D Coys carried out training after scheme had been approved by the Commanding Officer. A+C Companies carried onto cleaning + repairing of the roads in G 24 d & H 19 c. Addendum to O.O. 8 to 15 issued at 1400.	b. b. 3.
G 24 d 4 4	26th		Companies paraded at 0900 for inspection. A+C Companies carried on with training and B+D Companies with repairing + cleaning the roads. The Commanding Officer inspected the Stretcher Bearers at 0930. Capt J. J. Johns took over Command of "C" Company. Defence Scheme and Addendum No 2 to O.O. No 15 issued.	No. b. 7.
G 24 d 4 4	27th		The Battalion paraded for Church Parade. Other Denominations at 0900 and C of E at 1000. The Officer Commanding "B+C" Coys and the 2nd in Command and of "A+D" Coys reconnoitred the ground shown in O.O. No 15 Addendum No 1 para.	b. b. 17

(A800) Wt. W1771/M2031 750,000 5/17 D D & L, London, B.C. Sch. 52 Forms/C2118/14

Army Form C. 2118.

WAR DIARY
or
INTELLIGENCE SUMMARY.
(Erase heading not required.)

B'n Duke of Wellington

Instructions regarding War Diaries and Intelligence Summaries are contained in F.S. Regs., Part II. and the Staff Manual respectively. Title pages will be prepared in manuscript.

Place	Date 1918	Hour	Summary of Events and Information	Remarks and references to Appendices
G 24 d 44	Sept 27th		Continued. Lt W. Fielden was transferred to "D" Coy and took over the Command from the 14th inst. At 14:30 the Battalion played the Rifle Bdes Section at Football.	W.L.7
G 24 d 44	28th		Companies paraded for inspection at 09:00. Inspection of web equipment at 11:30. The Battalion formed a Section to the whole Battalion on Yellow area Sqn. The Commanding Officer, The Brigade Gas Officer inspected Gas Saw at 10:30.	W.L.7
G 24 d 44	29th		A "C" "D" Coys carried on training and "B" Coy carried on with Lecture Scheme. Lewis Gun Class, Signallers and Scouts carried on training under their respective specialist officers.	W.L.7
G 24 d 44	30th		A "B" "D" Coys carried on training carried on training and "C" Coy carried out Tactical Scheme. Lewis Gun Class, Signallers and Scouts carried on training under the respective specialist officers. All officers paraded under the Commanding officer at 15:00 to carry out a Tactical Scheme. Capt R.H. Bond reported from 59th Divisional School and took over Command of "D" Coy. Reinforcements 4.5 O.R's from Base. Lt W.H. Sweet M.R.C. relieved Capt F.R. Irwin with R.A.M.C. for duty.	W.L.7
G 24 d 44	31st		A, B, & C Coys carried on training under Coy arrangements and "D" Coy carried out Tactical Scheme. Lewis Gun Class, Signallers & Scouts carried on training under the respective Specialist officers. The new draft and all men in the Battalion were inspected by the Medical Officer.	W.L.7

R.J Shuss Lt.Col.

CONFIDENTIAL.

WAR DIARY

OF

13" Duke of Wellingtons West Riding Regt.

NOVEMBER 1918.

November 1918   13th B" Duke of Wellington Regt.   Army Form C. 2118.

WAR DIARY
or
INTELLIGENCE SUMMARY.
(Erase heading not required.)

Place	Date	Hour	Summary of Events and Information	Remarks and references to Appendices
Ref Sheet 39 1/40000 G24 d44 ½	Nov 1st 1918		Strength Officers 36. O.R's 742. The day was devoted to training	to 6.2.7.1.
"	2nd		The day was devoted to training	to 6.2.7.1.
"	3rd		Church Parade. 2/Lt H.C Marshall proceeded to England on leave.	to 6.2.7.1.
"	4th		The day was devoted to training. Lt W FIELDEN awarded the Military Cross.	to 6.2.7.1.
"	5th		Training - The Revd Capt J.A.R D MARSHALL. C.F. Reported for duty	to 6.2.7.1.
"	6th		Training - 11 Other Ranks awarded Military Medal. Major J.A. RODDICK. M.C. proceeded on Special leave to England.	to 6.2.7.1.
"	7th		Training - Capt- J. F. JOHNS proceeded to England on leave.	to 6.2.7.1.

November 1918

WAR DIARY 13th. Bn. Duke of Wellington's Army Form C. 2118.
or
INTELLIGENCE SUMMARY. Regt.

Place	Date	Hour	Summary of Events and Information	Remarks and references to Appendices
Rft Sect 37 Nouvu G24 d4.4.8	Nov 1918 8		The Battalion relieved the 15th Essex Regiment in the line Batn. H.Q. CHATEAU. I.19.c.	A.L.3
CHATEAU I.19.c	9		Patrols having reported front clear of the enemy the Battalion marched to Col LIEFFARD I.9.C.5.1 thence to Fré de la MOTTE and Battalion Head Quarters were established at J.12.d.0.9.	A.L.3
J.12.d.0.9.	10		Operation Order No 20 issued. Battalion marched to BROYERE. Battalion Head Quarters to 4.a.7.8.	A.L.3
4.a.9.8.	11		Armistice Signed.	A.L.3
L.a.9.8.	12		Battalion marched to PELAINES. Battalion Head Quarters No 74 Billet J.18.d.8.6	A.L.3
J.18.d.8.6	13 & 14		Training and cleaning up. P.+B.T. Musketry Gas Drill	A.L.3

November 1918.

WAR DIARY
INTELLIGENCE SUMMARY.

13th Bn. Duke of Wellington's Regt
Army Form C. 2118.

Place	Date	Hour	Summary of Events and Information	Remarks and references to Appendices
Ref Sheet 37 1/40000	Nov 1918			
J.19 d 8.6	15		The Battalion left VELAINES and marched one FAUCHY - BURGOYNE - REJET DU SART - CASLIÉTARD - Ponton Bridge J.14 C 6.3. - HULANS. Battalion Head Quarters H.26 C 6.6.	W.L.F
H.26 C 6.6	16		The Battalion left HULANS and marched to VILLEMS. Battalion Head Quarters M 5 d 4.1.	W.L.F
M.5 d 41	17.		The Battalion marched to Pt RONCHIN. Battalion Head Quarters Q.22 C.5.7. (Ref Sheet 36 1/40000). 2/Lt F OLDROYD Jr rejoined the Battalion	W.L.F
Ref Sheet 36. 1/40000 Q.22 C 5.7	18		Companies at disposal of company commanders for cleaning of equipment clothing and billets	13RHW Cmd
Q.22 C 5.7	19	10.00	The Brigadier General 148 Brigade inspected 13 Battalion. After Inspection training under company commanders	13RHW Cmd

WAR DIARY 1/5 Duke of Wellington's Regt

Army Form C. 2118.

INTELLIGENCE SUMMARY.

November 1918

Place	Date	Hour	Summary of Events and Information	Remarks and references to Appendices
Ref Sheet 36b NOYON				
Q.22.c.5.7	20	30	Ordinary Battalion Training carried out	RHQ Copy
Q.22.c.5.7	21		2nd Lt W. FIELDING M.C. awarded bar to Military Cross	
Q.22.c.5.7	27		2nd Lt C.D. JENKINS & 2nd Lt E. HOLMAN reported from Base for duty	RHQ Copy
Q.22.c.5.7	29		2nd Lt E.A. WAREING and 2nd Lt F. FEAVIOUR reported from base for duty. 2nd Lt L.W. FIELDING reported for duty from Hospital.	RHQ Copy

(J. Hall) Lt Col.
Comdg. 13th Duke of Wellington's Regt

WAR DIARY
INTELLIGENCE SUMMARY

13th Duke of Wellingtons Regt.

Army Form C. 2118.

Place	Date	Hour	Summary of Events and Information	Remarks and references to Appendices
Reft. Sheet 36 Jug. 100 Q.22.c.5.7	Dec 1st		Strength Officers 39. O.Rs. 938. Mr. F.J. Curtis posted from Base	F.F.1.
"	2nd		Training under Coy. arrangements. Capt. W. R. E. Hunt returned from France leave Movement orders issued for transport to proceed to BRUAY to U.K.	AP1
"	3rd		Training under Coy. arrangements. Transport proceeded to BRUAY at 08.00. Movement orders issued for Battalion to move to BRUAY 2/Lt. H.F. Denton on leave to U.K.	AP1
Reft Sheet 44 B K.20.a.a2	4th		Battalion moved by Bus to BRUAY at 05.00 — arrived 14.45. Transport line Ft. 24. b. 9.9. Major G.A. Redstick "Reinducted to Hospital	AP1
"	5th		Training under Coy. arrangements.	AP1
"	6th		Training under Coy. arrangements. Court of Enquiry Held re absence without leave of:- L/Cpl Raout G.T. 49403 — 'A' Coy. Pte. J. Brenard. Pte. Rea W. 2/Lt. K.A. Connor 49405 — D Coy 2/Lt. E. Holman	AP1

WAR DIARY
INTELLIGENCE SUMMARY

Army Form C. 2118.

13th Duke of Wellington's Regt.

Place	Date	Hour	Summary of Events and Information	Remarks and references to Appendices
Rt. fret HD Qrs K.20.a.6.2	7th		Training routine. Coy. arrangements. Enemy Enquiry / reconnoitres. Major G.A. Roddick M.C. discharged from Hospital. Movement order issued for relieving party to DUNKIRK.	N.T.T.
"	8th		'A' Coy & details left BRUAY at 11.00 - arrived CROIX RICOURT at 14.30 - entrained & left at 23.30	N.T.T.
frest A.N.W H.I.C.14.4	9th		'A' Coy & details arrived DUNKIRK at 05.00 Batt. H.Q. at 10.45 Capt. J.T.G. Hare Kane & U.K.	N.T.T.
"	10th		Fatigue parties on Demolished Camp (MARDYCK CAMP)	N.T.T.
"	11th		Remainder of Battalion arrives 06.30. (left BRUAY at 16.00 - arrived DUNKIRK 22.00.) entrained at 19.40) entrained at 04.50	N.T.T.
"	12th 13th		Fatigue - Camp. Constructing huts	N.T.T.
"	14th		Fatigues in Camp. Constructing huts. 2. M. Lieut F.D. Saunders admitted to Hospital.	N.T.T.

WAR DIARY
INTELLIGENCE SUMMARY

Army Form C. 2118.

13⁰ Duke of Wellington's Regt

Place	Date	Hour	Summary of Events and Information	Remarks and references to Appendices
19. N.W. C.44	Dec 15		Battalion (less 'C' Coy) fatigues in camp. 'C' Coy work on huts - debuses at R.S.F. Camp. 2/Lt. R.K. Harmon took over duties as Q.M. in absence of Q.M. Mr F.W. Saunders in hospital	N.T.R.
"	16⁰ cont.		Lt. G.J. Nobett R.A.S.C. joined from Base (attached) Capt. A. Banks M.C. rejoined from 59ᵈ Division - posted to 118 ᵈ Inf. Bde. H.Q.	N.T.R.
"	16⁰		Fatigue in camp constructing huts. 2/Lt. R.P. Stirling returned from leave to U.K. " F.M. Fawcett " " " " " J. Hodgson " " " "	N.T.R.
"	17⁰		Camp fatigue. Construction	N.T.R.
"	18⁰		Camp fatigue. Construction. Capt. P.M. Bond admitted to hospital	N.T.R.
"	19⁰		Camp fatigue. Construction. 2/Lt. G. Huntley leave to U.K. 1/Lt. R.B.A. Harrison relieved of duties of Q.M. by 2/Lt. J. Hodgson during absence of Q.M. in hospital. Capt. A.G. Upton returned from 5 ᵈ Army Musketry School - posted to 'D' Coy.	N.T.R.

29 APR 1919
YORK

WAR DIARY
INTELLIGENCE SUMMARY
(Erase heading not required.)

1/3 Duke of Wellington - Reg.t

Army Form C. 2118.

Place	Date	Hour	Summary of Events and Information	Remarks and references to Appendices
Sheet 19. N.W. Cor. H.I.C.4.4	20th Dec		Camp fatigue - Construction	
			2/Lt. M. Brooks M.M.; 2/Lt. R.S. Turney,	
			2/Lt. R.S. Turnbull - leave to U.K.	
"	21st		Battalion in camp - Construction	
			Tp. Q.M. F.M. Saunders discharged from hospital.	
"	22nd		Company fatigues - Construction. Divine Service.	
			2/Lt. R.L. Denton from leave to U.K.	
			" B.K. Brewill leave to U.K.	
"	23rd		Camp fatigues - Construction.	
"	24th		Camp fatigues - Construction.	
			2/Lt. J. Hodgson admitted to hospital	
"	25th		Xmas day. Divine Service	
			Capt P.M. Bond returned from hospital	
"	26th		Camp fatigues - Constructing huts.	
			2/Lt. F. Oldroyd; Lt. D.F. McFall; 2/Lt. D.K.M. Hairsten; leave to U.K.	
			Lt. R.A. Connors leave to Le Havre.	

Army Form C. 2118.

WAR DIARY
or
INTELLIGENCE SUMMARY.
(Erase heading not required.)

13 Duke of Wellington's Rgt.

Instructions regarding War Diaries and Intelligence Summaries are contained in F. S. Regs., Part II. and the Staff Manual respectively. Title pages will be prepared in manuscript.

No 2 INFANTRY RECORDS · 29 APR 1919 · YORK

Place	Date	Hour	Summary of Events and Information	Remarks and references to Appendices
West of N.W. Div. H.S.C. 4.4	26th		Const. fatigues. Construction	N.T.J.
"	26th		Const. fatigues. Construction. Capt. J.J. Brennand home to U.K.	N.T.J.
"	29th		Divine Service. Court of Enquiry was held if force loss of bicycle + set of harness. President Capt. T. A. Upton. Members S/Lt. J.M. Tarrett. " J.K. Fever.	N.T.J.
"	30th		Const. fatigues. Construction.	N.T.J.
"	31st		Const. fatigues. Construction.	N.T.J.

J. Wilbraham Major Comdg
13 West Riding Regt.

(A5001) Wt. W17271/M2031 750,000 5/17 D. D. & L., London, E.C. Sch. 52 Forms/C2118/14

PF

WAR DIARY 13th Battn. Duke of Wellington's Regt.
or
INTELLIGENCE SUMMARY.

Army Form C. 2118.

102

Place	Date	Hour	Summary of Events and Information	Remarks and references to Appendices
H.I.C.40 N.W.	1919 Jan 1		Major J.A. Roddick, M.C. assumed temporary command of Battn; in absence of Lt. Col. P.S. Hall, D.S.O. evacuated to Hospital. 2/Lt. G. W. Stricken leave to U.K. Battn turned out under arms. Disorder amongst N.Z.R. (Maoris). Strength — Officers 38 O.R.'s 733.	CDJ
"	2nd		Lt. & Q.M. F.W. Saunders leave to U.K. Battn; turned out under arms - on patrol.	CDJ
"	3rd		Lt. R.A. Garner rejoined from leave to K. Saune. Camps fatigues. Construction. Lt. W. Fielden, M.C., leave to U.K.	CDJ
"	4th		Camp fatigues. — Construction. 2/Lt. E. Sexton takes over duties of A/Q.M. during the absence of Q.M. 1/Lt. F W Saunders on leave to U.K. 2/Lt. P.J. Godfrey to Embarkation Camp for Demob.	CDJ
"	5th		Divine Service. — Camp fatigues — Construction. 2/Lt. A. Huntly returned from. U.K. leave.	CDJ
			Camp fatigues. — Construction 2/Lt. H. Bristow M.M. & Lt. J. Turner, R.J. Turnbull returned from leave U.K. — Lt. Col. P.S. Hall, D.S.O. from Hospital.	CDJ

WAR DIARY
or
INTELLIGENCE SUMMARY.

13th Battn Duke of Wellington's Regt Army Form C. 2118.

(Erase heading not required.)

Instructions regarding War Diaries and Intelligence Summaries are contained in F. S. Regs., Part II. and the Staff Manual respectively. Title pages will be prepared in manuscript.

Place	Date 1919	Hour	Summary of Events and Information	Remarks and references to Appendices
Sheet 19. N.W. H.1.C.4.4	Jan 7th		Camp Fatigues. – Construction. Major J.H. Roddick M.C. relinquishes Command of Battn. on Jan. 5th on the return of Lt. Col. P.S. Hall, D.S.O. from hospital, who resumed command from Jan. 6th.	CDH
"	8th		Camp Fatigues. – Construction.	CDH
"	9th		Working parties. – Construction. – 2/Lt. H.P. Skipping takes over Command of "B" Coy. Lt. R.A. Connor leave to U.K. 2/Lt. A.S. King leave to U.K.	CDH
"	10th		Working parties. – Construction.	CDH
"	11th		Working parties. – Construction.	CDH
"	12th		Divine Service. – Lt. MacDuff from leave U.K. – also 2/Lt. D.R.H. Harrison.	CDH
"	13th		Working parties. – Construction.	CDH
"	14th		Working parties. – Construction.	CDH
"	15th		Working parties. – Construction.	CDH
"	16th		Working parties. – Construction. – M.O. on leave (France).	CDH
"	17th		Working parties. – Construction.	CDH

WAR DIARY or INTELLIGENCE SUMMARY

Army Form C. 2118.

13th Battn. Duke of Wellington's Regt.

Place	Date	Hour	Summary of Events and Information	Remarks and references to Appendices
Sheet 19 N.W. H.I.C.4.4	1919 Jan. 18th		Working parties. Camp Construction. 2/Lt. F.S. Desroys from leave U.K. Lt. B.A. Brewill " "	ODE
"	19th		Divine Service	ODE
"	20th		Working parties — Camp Construction. L/Cpl. F.G.M. Jefferies, Pte. W.J. Shepherd, W. Whiting, P. Simpson, J. Needham " "	ODE
"	21st		Working parties — Camp Construction.	ODE
"	22nd		Working parties — Camp Construction. — Lt. R.A. Connor returned from leave U.K.	ODE
"	23rd		Battalion working Demobilisation Camp. Lt. Col. P.S. Hall, D.S.O. to Hospital. Lt. W. Fielder, M.C., returned from leave U.K. 2/Lt. G.W. Tricker " "	ODE
"	24th		Battalion working Demobilisation Camp.	ODE
"	25th		Battalion working Demobilisation Camp. 2/Lt. A.S. King returned from leave U.K. L/Cpl. J.M. & Pte. W. Dean " "	ODE
"	26th		Voluntary Divine Service for men not employed on Demob: Camp. Major S.A. Upton & Capt. W. Fleming to Hospital. Capt. C. Webb M.C. & J. Furgland joined Battn. & taken on strength	ODE

WAR DIARY 13th Batt. Duke of Wellingtons. Regt.

INTELLIGENCE SUMMARY

Army Form C. 2118.

(Erase heading not required.)

Place	Date	Hour	Summary of Events and Information	Remarks and references to Appendices
Sheet 19. N.W. H.1.C.4.4.	1919 Jan 27th		Battalion working Demob: Camp. Bn Transport (Horses) attached to 516 Coy, R.A.S.C. for Rations from 1900 hrs today	
"	28th		Battalion working Demob Camp. Lt R Gammon to Hospital 2/Lt L R Purviss from Hospital	
"	29th		Battalion working Demob Camp Lt Col P. S. Hall D.S.O. from Hospital 2/Lt H.T Denton att'd 516 Coy R.A.S.C.	
"	30th		Battalion working Demob Camp	
"	31st		Battalion working Demob Camp	

B.S. Hall Lt Col
Comdg
13th West Riding Regt

WAR DIARY 13th Duke of Wellingtons Regt Army Form C. 2118.
or
INTELLIGENCE SUMMARY.
(Erase heading not required.)

WO/10

Place	Date	Hour	Summary of Events and Information	Remarks and references to Appendices
Sheet 19 N.W.	July 1919 1st		Battalion working Demob Camp Strength - Officers 36. O.R's 540	
	2nd		Battalion working Demob Camp Voluntary Period Service for men not employed	
	3rd		Battalion working Demob Camp	
	4th		Battalion working Demob Camp A/CAPT. W.M. FLAXINGTON & LT. R.A. CONNOR from Hospital	
	5th		Battalion working Demob Camp	
	6th		Battalion working Demob Camp 2/LT R.J. TURNBULL to Embarkation Camp	
	7th		Battalion working Demob Camp 2/LT W.H.T. TURNER to Embarkation Camp	
	8th		Battalion working Demob Camp A/MAJOR R.H. BOND to Embarkation Camp	
	9th		Battalion working Demob Camp Voluntary Period Service for men not employed Presentation of Medals by Major General SMYTHE V.C. C.B. to A/CAPT FIELDEN, MC & bar, & SGT TURNER D.C.M. A/L.CPL. FLOYD on leave to U.K.	

Army Form C. 2118.

WAR DIARY
or
INTELLIGENCE SUMMARY.

13th Duke of Wellingtons Regt.

(Erase heading not required.)

Place	Date	Hour	Summary of Events and Information	Remarks and references to Appendices
Sheet 19 NW	1919 10th		Battalion working Demob Camp	CM
	11th		Battalion working Demob Camp. 212 reinforcements reported from 1/6th Battn Duke of Wellingtons Regt.	CM
	12th		Battalion working Demob Camp The following Officers reported from leave for duty:- LT. S.P. DORMAN. 2/LT H. MILNES. LT A. WHITEHEAD M.C. A/CAPT. H. SMITH 2/LT H.C.J. WOODROW. 2/LT J.J. BLIGHT. LT G.S. BALDICK. 2/LT C.E.W. ROGERS. 2/LT. C.A. WAREING leave to UK	CM
	13th		Battalion working Demob Camp	CM
	14th		Battalion working Demob Camp CAPT J.A.R.D. MARSHALL leave to UK	CM
	15th		Battalion working Demob Camp 88 Reinforcements reported from 1/4 Battn Duke of Wellingtons Regt The following Officers reported for duty LT. A. MALLALIEU. 2/LT R.R. RAINFORD	CM
	16th		Battalion working Demob Camp Divine Service (Voluntary) for men not on duty	CM

Army Form C. 2118.

WAR DIARY
or
INTELLIGENCE SUMMARY. 13th Duke of Wellingtons Regt

(Erase heading not required.)

Place	Date	Hour	Summary of Events and Information	Remarks and references to Appendices
Sheet 19 N.W.	1919 17th		Battalion working Pensob Camp. The following Officer reported for duty - 2/Lt F W KELTIE	CRA
	18th		Battalion working Pensob Camp	CRA
	19th		Battalion working Pensob Camp	CRA
	20th		Battalion working Pensob Camp. Lt R.A CONNOR took over command of "C" Coy 2/Lt H.C.MARSHALL to Hospital	CRA
	21st		Battalion working Pensob Camp. The following Officers reported for duty 2/Lt H.PLANT 2/Lt H. HUDSON. 2/Lt A V WHALLEY. LT H DAWSON	CRA
	22nd		Battalion working Pensob Camp 2/LT BRISTOW to Hospital	CRA
	23rd		Battalion working Pensob Camp	CRA
	24th		Battalion working Pensob Camp	CRA
	25th		Battalion working Pensob Camp. The following Officer reported for duty - LT & QMSTR WILLIAMS.	CRA

Army Form C. 2118.

WAR DIARY
or
INTELLIGENCE SUMMARY.
(Erase heading not required.)

13th Duke of Wellington's Regt

Instructions regarding War Diaries and Intelligence Summaries are contained in F. S. Regs., Part II. and the Staff Manual respectively. Title pages will be prepared in manuscript.

Place	Date	Hour	Summary of Events and Information	Remarks and references to Appendices
Sheet 19 N W	1919 26th		Battn working Pinnel Camp. LT COL R.S HALL leave to U.K. 2/LT. H.C MARSHALL from Hospital A/Capt Flexington leave to U.K. A/MAJOR. JOHNS assumed command of Battn in absence of Lt Col Hall leave to U.K.	✓ ✓
"	27th		Battn working Pinnel Camp 2/LT BRISTOW from Hospital	✓
"	28th		Battn working Pinnel Camp 2/LT C.A WAREING from leave to U.K. 248 Reinforcements reported from 1/4. 1/6 & 1/14 Battns Duke of Wellingtons Regt The following Officers reported for duty 2/LT R LEDDRA, LT J FLETCHER, 2/LT H.C DE MAINE, 2/LT R.C WILLIAMS 2/LT T. BUCKLER, LT E.W DIMES, 2/LT R.E JONES, 2/LT V BIDDLE, 2/LT H.R NEWMAN	✓

[signature] MAJOR
13 Duke of Wellingtons Regt

59 DIVISION
178 INFY BDE

Duke of Wellington's
13TH BN (WEST RIDING REGT)

MARCH & APRIL 1919

MISSING

Army Form C. 2118.

WAR DIARY
INTELLIGENCE SUMMARY. 13th Duke of Wellington's (W.R.) Regt.

(Erase heading not required.)

Place	Date	Hour	Summary of Events and Information	Remarks and references to Appendices
Sheet 19 N.W	May 1919			
	1		Battn working Demob Camp. Capt Webb to UK for Demob. 2/Lt Wayte & B Wayte D.S. to Bn. Col W. Hall P.S.O. Battalion from Bn to Bde taken over command of	
	2		Battn working Demob Camp. Capt Yorke 2/Lt Smith 2/Lt Yeats joined for duty from UK West Yorks. Capt Gubay to Divisional School & also 2/Lt Baldrick from leave to UK	
	3		Battn working Demob Camp. Lt Fitzpatrick & party Lt Fitzpatrick 2/Lt Auty joined for duty from UK. West Yorks. Lt Newman leave to UK. 2/Lt Rainford from leave to UK	
	4		Battn working Demob Camp. Funeral of Gunner Lt Bottrall P.S.O. to UK to evacuation. Capt McTool from leave to UK	
	5		Battn working Demob Camp. Funeral of Mr Hardy of 2/Lt Priniville leave to UK	
	6		Battn working Demob Camp. A Coy training. 2/Lt Denton & Lt Milnes from leave to UK	
	7		Battn working Demob Camp. A Coy training	
	8		Battn working Demob Camp. Inspection of A Coy by C.O.	
	9		Battn working Demob Camp. 2/Lt Gun P.C. to UK for leave. Capt Smith legns to UK. 2/Lt Harnen from leave to UK. 2/Lt Buckler to Hospital	
	10		Battn working Demob Camp. 2/Lt Ryder from leave to UK. 2/Lt Savayds M.M. from Divisional School & also	
	11		Battn working Demob Camp Parade Divine Service. Capt Connor from leave to Rome	
	12		Battn working Demob Camp. B Coy training. 2/Lt Dawson P.C. to UK for leave 2/Lt H C du Mriny & 2/Lt Turner leave leg UK	
	13		Battn working Demob Camp. Battn inspection by C.O. B Coy training	
	14		Battn working Demob Camp. B Coy training	12.Z 3 sheets

Army Form C. 2118.

WAR DIARY
or
INTELLIGENCE=SUMMARY.
(Erase heading not required.)

13th DOW (WR) Regt

Instructions regarding War Diaries and Intelligence Summaries are contained in F.S. Regs., Part II. and the Staff Manual respectively. Title pages will be prepared in manuscript.

Place	Date May 1919	Hour	Summary of Events and Information	Remarks and references to Appendices
Shut 19 NW	15		Battn working Trench camp	
	16		13 boy training	AM
			Battn working Trench camp 13 boy training	
	17		Attest Draught to UK for repatriation	AM
			Battn working Trench camp. 13 boy expected by 10 to U. 8/Lt	
			Harding found for duty from Hospital & apt Holditch 9/Lt	AB
			Hollings from leave to UK	
	18		Battn station Trench camp	
			Parade Divine Service	AB
	19		Battn working Trench camp	AB
	20		Boy training Trench camp	
			Battn working Trench camp	AB
	21		& boy training	
			Battn working Trench camp & boy training	
			2/Lt Buckles from Hospital	AM
	22		Battn working Trench camp & boy training 2/Lt Harris to hospital	AM
			2/Lt Loudon to UK Draft Conductor for Leave	AM
	23		Battn working Trench camp	
			Boy training	AM
	24		Battn working Trench camp & 2/Lt Luck back from leave to UK	
			Boy training Rev. Capt R. Murray leave to UK	AM
	25		Battn working Trench camp Murray 2/into service a/Lt Woolnys	AM
			to UK for Trench Draft 2/Lt thurcher from leave to UK	
	26		Battn working Draught to Paris & boy training	AM
			from Leave to UK	
	27		Battn working Trench Camp & boy training 2/Lt HC de Morris	AM
			from leave to UK 2/Lt Fletcher DC to UK	
	28		Battn working Trench camp & boy training	AM
			from leave to UK	
	29		Battn working Trench camp	AM
			& boy training	

Army Form C. 2118.

WAR DIARY
or
INTELLIGENCE SUMMARY. 13th Duke of Wellington (W.R.) Regt
(Erase heading not required.)

Place	Date	Hour	Summary of Events and Information	Remarks and references to Appendices
Rue 19 N.W.	May 29		Battn working Parade & Coste Parades for Musketry & Bathing.	M.
	30			
	31		Battn working Parade & Coy Inspection at 6 by 2/Lt	Copy

OBarton
Major
Comdg 13th D.O.W. (W.R.) Regt

59 DIVISION
178 INFY BDE
DUKE OF WELLINGTON'S
13TH BN (WEST RIDING REGT)

JUNE 1919
MISSING

D.A.G.,
G.H.Q.,
3rd. E C H E L O N.
****

> HEADQUARTERS,
> 178TH
> INFANTRY BRIGADE.
>
> No. ....
> Date. 14/8/19

Herewith find War Diaries for Month of July 1919.

14th AUGUST 1919.

Brigadier - General,
Commanding 178th Infantry Brigade.

13th Duke of Wellingtons (W R) Regt

Army Form C. 2118

WAR DIARY
or
INTELLIGENCE SUMMARY
(Erase heading not required.)

95 15

Place	Date	Hour	Summary of Events and Information	Remarks and references to Appendices
SHEET 19 N.W.	July 1		Guard Duties Dunkirk & Bergues a/c Capt F Wedan M.C. to U.K. to demob. 2/Lt Hudson leave to U.K	App
	2		Guard Duties Dunkirk & Bergues	App
	3		do	App
	4		do	App
	5		do	App
	6		Guard Duties Dunkirk & Bergues. Divine Service	App
	7		Guard Duties Dunkirk & Bergues. Lt Dorman & 2/Lt proceeded from leave to UK	App
	8		Guard Duties Dunkirk & Bergues. Lt Dorman to ZENEGHEM. Capt Jacks from leave to U.K.	App
	9		Guard Duties Dunkirk & Bergues. Lt Girl & Lt Cushy leave to U.K.	App
	10		Guard Duties Dunkirk & Bergues. Major Hutchinson reported from UK for duty & assumes 2nd in Command	App
	11		Guard Duties Dunkirk & Bergues	App
	12		do	App
	13		Guard Duties Dunkirk & Bergues. Divine Service	App
	14		Guard Duties Dunkirk & Bergues. General Holiday (French Peace Celb.)	App
	15		Guard Duties Dunkirk & Bergues. Capt Beckwith from leave to U.K.	App
	16		Guard Duties Dunkirk & Bergues. 2/Lt Burgess & Mant & Lt Stephenson & St Jacques to 2/6th D.L.I. 2/Lt Burchip, Lt Mant, Lt Stephenson & St Jacques on leave to UK	App 13/2 sheet

WAR DIARY 13th Duke of Wellingtons (West Riding) Regt.
Army Form C. 2118.

INTELLIGENCE SUMMARY
(Erase heading not required.)

Instructions regarding War Diaries and Intelligence Summaries are contained in F. S. Regs., Part II. and the Staff Manual respectively. Title pages will be prepared in manuscript.

Place	Date	Hour	Summary of Events and Information	Remarks and references to Appendices
SHEET 19 NW	July 17		Guard Duties Punkish & Beynes. Major Reuben to UK for 6 mos.	CR
	18		Guard Duties Punkish & Beynes	CR
	19		2/Lt W Ritchies Reported. 2/Lt Hewitt to UK after leave	CR
	20		Guard Duties Punkish & Beynes. Stores to Gibraltar Guard Duties	CR
			2/Lt Agoptiah leaves to UK Beynes.	CR
			Divine Service	CR
	21		Friends at Punkish & Beynes relieved by N.F.s & R.S.F.s	CR
	22		Battalion Sports (Postponed) 2/Lt Knowson from leave to UK	CR
	23		Battalion Sports	CR
	24		Guard Duties Punkish & Beynes 2/Lt Williams leave to UK	CR
	25		Guard Duties Punkish & Beynes 2/Lt Jones leave to UK	CR
	26		Guard Duties Punkish & Beynes. 2/Lt Kedoha leave to UK	CR
	27		Guard Duties Punkish & Beynes. Divine Service	CR
	28		Guard Duties Punkish & Beynes 2/Lt Yeats from leave to UK	CR
	29		Guard Duties Punkish & Beynes. 2/Lt Duty from leave to UK	CR
	30		Guard Duties Punkish & Beynes	CR
	31		Guard Duties Punkish & Beynes. 2/Lt Smith from leave to UK	CR

AWayte
Comdg 13th P.O.W. (W.R) Regt
Lt Col

To: The Secretary

WAR OFFICE (S.D.2)

Herewith Original Copy of the War Diary of this Unit, for the month of AUGUST 1919, sent to you in accordance with G.R.O. 7263 of 29.8.1919.

[signature]
p/r Lt. Col.

1.9.1919.   Cmdg. 13th Bn. Duke of Wellington's (W.R.) Regt.

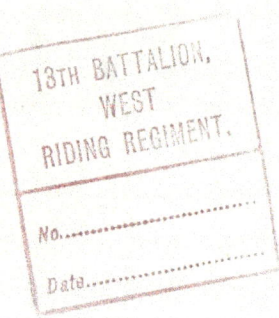

WAR DIARY
or
INTELLIGENCE SUMMARY.
(Erase heading not required.)

13th Bn Duke of Wellington (W.R. Regt)

Army Form C. 2118.

Place	Date	Hour	Summary of Events and Information	Remarks and references to Appendices
Sheet 19 N.W	August 1st		Guard Futuo Dunkish & Beyeus. Rehearsal for G.O.C. inspection. Lt Whitehead MC. fired leave to U.K.	
	2		Guard Futuo Dunkwh & Beyeus. Inspection of the Battalion by the G.O.C. in full marching order.	
	3		Guard Futuo Dunkwh & Beyeus. Divine Service.	
	4		Guard Futuo Dunkwh & Beyeus. Bayonet fighting.	
	5		Guard Futuo Dunkwh & Beyeus. Inspection of transport by O.C. 2Lt Bob Wayte & S.O. leave to U.K. Major Hutchinson M.C. assumed command. Lt Pickles leave to U.K. Circular relief of companies 2/Lt Hayslip from leave to U.K.	
	6		Guard Futuo Dunkwh & Beyeus	
	7		Guard Futuo Dunkwh & Beyeus 2/Lt Royer from leave to U.K.	
	8		Guard Futuo Dunkwh & Beyeus 2Lt Maddle leave to U.K.	
	9		Guard Futuo Dunkwh & Beyeus	
	10		Guard Futuo Dunkwh & Beyeus from Service	
	11		Guard Futuo Dunkwh & Beyeus Lt Whatley leave to U.K. (contd)	

Army Form C. 2118.

WAR DIARY
or
INTELLIGENCE SUMMARY.
(Erase heading not required.)

13th Bn Duke of Wellington's (W R) Regt

Instructions regarding War Diaries and Intelligence Summaries are contained in F. S. Regs., Part II. and the Staff Manual respectively. Title pages will be prepared in manuscript.

Place	Date	Hour	Summary of Events and Information	Remarks and references to Appendices
Rest 19 NW	12		Guard Duties Dunkirk & Reninghe	
	13		Guard Duties Dunkirk & Reninghe 4/Lt Jones to St Germain prior to OR on draft Reinf to UK Officers 4/Lt Rickles leave to UK	
	14		Guard Duties Dunkirk & Reninghe 8/Lt Woodrow Leys to UK Lt Col Rylston Hampshire Regt assumes command of Battalion	
	15		Guard Duties Dunkirk & Reninghe	
	16		Guard Duties Dunkirk & Reninghe	
	17		Guard Duties Dunkirk & Reninghe 7/Lt Blyth leave to UK	
	18		Guard Duties Dunkirk & Reninghe Capt Gibney MC assumes command of A Coy	
	19		Guard Duties Dunkirk & Reninghe	
	20		Guard Duties Dunkirk & Reninghe Lt Fletcher leave to UK	
	21		Guard Duties Dunkirk & Reninghe	
	22		Guard Duties Dunkirk & Reninghe	
	23		Guard Duties Dunkirk & Reninghe (contd)	

Army Form C. 2118.

WAR DIARY
or
INTELLIGENCE SUMMARY.
(Erase heading not required.) 13th Bn Duke of Wellington (W.R.) Regt

Instructions regarding War Diaries and Intelligence Summaries are contained in F. S. Regs., Part II. and the Staff Manual respectively. Title pages will be prepared in manuscript.

Place	Date	Hour	Summary of Events and Information	Remarks and references to Appendices
Bat HQrs 19	August 24		2nd Lieut Dunkirk & Bynins Lt Widnes on mob leave to UK. 2/Lt Andrell from leave to UK Prison Service	
	25		2nd Lieuts Dunkirk & Bynins 2/Lt Reinford leave to UK	
	26		2nd Lieuts Dunkirk & Bynins. 53 Party men left for demobilization	
	27		2nd Lieuts Dunkirk & Bynins 2/Lt Hunter from Hospital 2/Lt Whalley from leave to UK 75 Party men left for demob.	
	28		2nd Lieuts Dunkirk & Bynins Lt Liddiard to Records UK Doctor Berand returned by 30th N.F.	
	29		2nd Lieuts Bynins Lts Rogers & Williams returned from command	
	30		Bynins Lieuts returned by 30th N.F. 2/Lt's Dispatch Hadi Osman Iroqui Plant returned from command 2/Lt Hunter leave to UK Prison Service	
	31			

Bondy 13 70 W (W.411) 3/6

Army Form C. 2118.

WAR DIARY
or
INTELLIGENCE SUMMARY
(Erase heading not required.) 13th Bn P.O.W. (W.R.) Regt.

Instructions regarding War Diaries and Intelligence Summaries are contained in F. S. Regs., Part II. and the Staff Manual respectively. Title pages will be prepared in manuscript.

Place	Date	Hour	Summary of Events and Information	Remarks and references to Appendices
Dunkirk Sheet 19 NW	Sept 1		Returning camp equipment to Ordnance.	CRB
	2		do	CRB
	3		do	CRB
	4		do	CRB
	5		do 2/Lt Blight from leave to UK	CRB
			Lt Jaques leave to UK	
			Lt Fletcher from leave to UK	
	6		do Battalion bonsire	CRB
	7		do 2/Lt Turner leave to UK	CRB
			Lt Snow to U.K leave to UK	
	8		do Lt Butler leave to UK	CRB
	9		do	CRB
	10		do	CRB
	11		do 2/Lt Rainford from leave to UK	CRB
	12		Preparing to embark for U.K.	CRB
	13		Bn embarked for U.K. at 14.00 hrs. Transport & equipment guard to follow.	CRB

13TH BATTALION.
WEST RIDING REGIMENT.
No. S934
Date 1.9.19

[signature] Lt Col
Comdg 13th POW (W.R.) Regt

www.ingramcontent.com/pod-product-compliance
Lightning Source LLC
Chambersburg PA
CBHW081450160426
43193CB00013B/2427